DISGUSTING ANIMAL DINNERS

Moths Drink Tears!

Miriam Coleman

PowerKiDS press™
New York

Published in 2014 by The Rosen Publishing Group, Inc.
29 East 21st Street, New York, NY 10010

First Edition

Editor: Joanne Randolph
Book Design: Kate Vlachos
Photo Research: Katie Stryker

Photo Credits: Cover Rob Hainer/Shutterstock.com; front cover (series title) © iStockphoto/lishenjun; back cover graphic -Albachiaraa-/Shutterstock.com; p. 4 Gucio_55/Shutterstock.com; p. 5 Jeff McGraw/Shutterstock.com; pp. 6–7, 14, 15 by Dr. Roland Hilgartner; p. 8 © iStockphoto.com/Giovanni Banfi; p. 9 Marut Matt Sillapasoontorn/Shutterstock.com; p. 10 Sue Robinson/Shutterstock.com; p. 11 Craig Taylor/Shutterstock.com; pp. 12–13 Photography by Shin.T/Flickr/Getty Images; p. 16–17 Katarina Christenson/Shutterstock.com; p. 18 Visuals Unlimited, Inc./Robert Pickett/Visuals Unlimited/Getty Images; pp. 19, 22 iStockphoto/Thinkstock; p. 20 2630ben/Shutterstock.com; p. 21 worldswildlifewonders/Shutterstock.com.

Library of Congress Cataloging-in-Publication Data

Coleman, Miriam.
Moths drink tears! / by Miriam Coleman. — First edition.
   pages cm. — (Disgusting animal dinners)
Includes index.
ISBN 978-1-4777-2883-3 (library) — ISBN 978-1-4777-2970-0 (pbk.) —
ISBN 978-1-4777-3043-0 (6-pack)
1. Moths—Juvenile literature. I. Title.
QL544.2.C652 2014
595.78—dc23
                                    2013022340

Manufactured in the United States of America

CPSIA Compliance Information: Batch #W14PK6: For Further Information contact Rosen Publishing, New York, New York at 1-800-237-9932

CONTENTS

Meet the Moth 4

Lachry-What? 6

Where in the World? 8

Sucking Up Tears 10

Disgusting Moth Facts! 12

Harpoon Tongue 14

Busy in the Night 16

Life Cycle 18

Diet 20

The Eyes Have It 22

Glossary 23

Index 24

Websites 24

Meet the Moth

Moths are winged insects that are close relatives of butterflies. Their wings are **delicate** and covered in tiny scales of different colors. There are at least 130,000 known **species** of moths, and they live all over the world.

Moths have compound eyes and antennae, or feelers, on their heads, as do many insects.

Some moths have patterns on their wings that look like eyes. These eyespots are likely meant to surprise would-be predators so the moth can get away.

Different types of moths eat different foods. Some moths eat leaves and others eat wood. You might even find moths in your kitchen eating your cereal or moths in your closet eating your coat. You might not like that, but it could be worse. Some moths feed on tears!

Lachry-What?

Moths that drink tears are called lachryphagous. This term comes from the Latin word *lacrima*, meaning "tear," and the Greek word *phago*, which means "eat." Why would an animal want to drink tears? Tears are made up of salt, water, and small amounts of **protein**. All of these things are necessary for a moth's survival.

Most lachryphagous moths drink tears from the eyes of large, gentle **mammals**, such as mules, water buffalo, elephants, and horses. Sometimes these moths will also drink tears from the eyes of people.

This lachryphagous moth is drinking the tears from a sleeping bird. These moths are also sometimes called eye-frequenting moths.

Where in the World?

Tear-drinking moths can be found in and around **tropical** parts of Africa, Asia, and South America as well as Australia. The greatest number of tear-drinking species can be found in areas where dry seasons are followed by very damp seasons.

This map shows the continents on which tear-drinking moths can be found.

Map of Where Tear-Drinking Moths Live

NORTH AMERICA

Atlantic Ocean

EUROPE

ASIA

AFRICA

Indian Ocean

Pacific Ocean

SOUTH AMERICA

Atlantic Ocean

AUSTRALIA

KEY

Where tear-drinking moths live

There are many tear-drinking species of moths in Thailand, shown here.

In Thailand, where heavy rains fall through the summer **monsoon** season, there are nearly 100 species of moths that drink tears.

Lachryphagous moths prefer to live in forests, but some live in open **pastures** next to forests. Several species live on the **savanna** in Africa.

Sucking Up Tears

You can clearly see the proboscis on this moth's mouth as it stretches it out to drink nectar from a flower.

Most species of adult moths feed through proboscises, long, thin tubes that grow out of their heads. Tear-drinking moths use their proboscises like straws to suck up the juice from the surface of animals' eyes.

One type of moth uses its proboscis to scrape its victims' eyes, causing the eyes to tear up and giving the moth more to drink. Other species might only tickle their victims. A type of moth that drinks elephant tears is so tiny and gentle that the elephants hardly even notice the moths.

This image shows a proboscis that is not in use. Moths, butterflies, and bees all roll up their proboscises when they are not feeding.

DISGUSTING MOTH FACTS!

1 The vampire moth can pierce the skin of an animal and drink its blood.

2 Some species of moths drink human sweat.

3 In most lachryphagous species, only the adult male moths will drink tears.

4 Moths may also cause eye diseases, such as pinkeye, in cattle and water buffalo, which can make the animals go blind.

5 One of the largest tear-drinking moths has a proboscis that is more than 1.5 inches (3.8 cm) long.

6 Several different kinds of moths feed by sucking at the skin sores on the undersides of elephants.

7 For some moths, diseased eyes provide the tears with the most **nutrients** because they contain extra white blood cells.

Harpoon Tongue

One type of moth that lives in the forests of Madagascar, a large island off the coast of Africa, drinks tears from the eyelids of sleeping birds. This is the only kind of moth known to drink birds' tears.

This moth has its proboscis under a bird's eyelid.

This close-up image of a tear-drinking moth's proboscis shows that it has sharp barbs on it that the moth can use to scrape the bird's eye to make it water.

These moths have proboscises that are shaped like harpoons, with hooks and barbs. The moth sits on the neck of a sleeping bird and sticks the proboscis under the bird's eyelids. The hooks and barbs help anchor the proboscis in place without waking up the bird, and the moth drinks its fill of the salty tears.

Busy in the Night

Unlike butterflies, most species of moths are nocturnal, which means that they are active in the nighttime. You might notice that as dark falls where you live, the moths come out.

For moths that feed on human tears, nighttime is a good time to eat since sleeping people will not swat them away. Many types of moths drink the tears of animals that keep their large eyes open at night and have no hands to swat the moths away.

Most moths come out at night to look for food. They hide and rest during the day.

Life Cycle

Moths begin life as eggs.

There are four stages in the life cycle of a moth. Moths start out as tiny eggs. The young that hatch from the eggs are called larvae, or caterpillars. The caterpillars have no wings and are soft, like worms. They eat as much as they can so that they can grow. Then they shed their old skin when it becomes too small.

When the caterpillar gets big enough, it becomes a pupa and its body starts to change. Most species spin themselves a cocoon, a little pouch that protects them while they change. Finally, the creature breaks out of the cocoon in the shape of an adult moth with wings. This kind of big change is called **metamorphosis**.

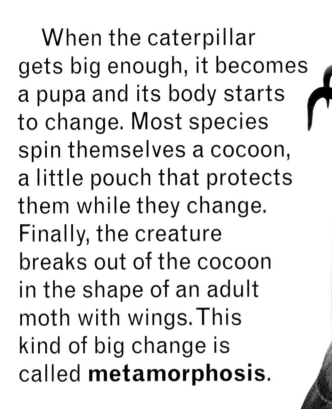

This is a moth just emerging from its cocoon.

Diet

While caterpillars munch their way through leaves and wood and other foods, most adult moths survive on a liquid diet. Many moths drink the nectar from flowers, tree sap, or liquid that comes out of rotting fruits and vegetables.

One species of tear-drinking moth, called *Mabra elephantofila*, prefers to dine on the tears of elephants, as its Latin name suggests.

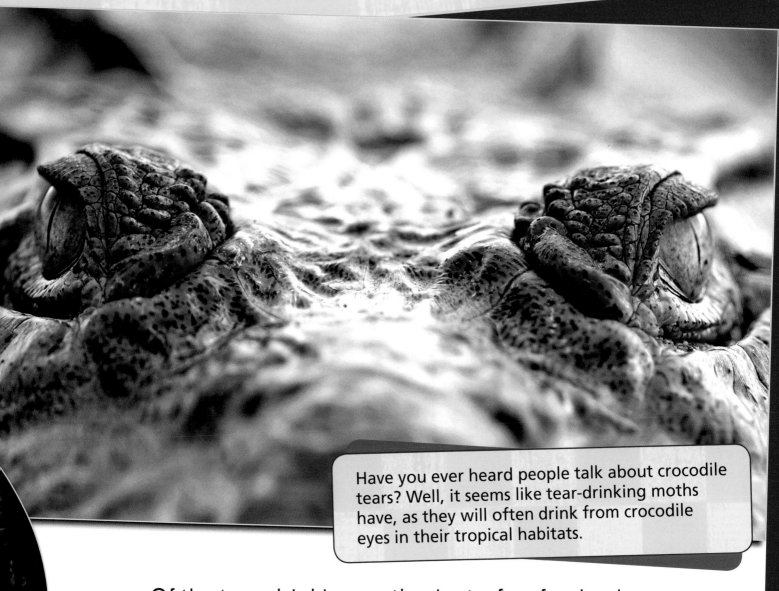

Have you ever heard people talk about crocodile tears? Well, it seems like tear-drinking moths have, as they will often drink from crocodile eyes in their tropical habitats.

Of the tear-drinking moths, just a few feed only on tears. Most of these moths also drink other bodily **fluids** from animals, including **saliva**, **mucus**, **urine**, and blood from wounds. While some moths will feed right from the animals' bodies, many species eat only fluids that the other animals leave behind on plants or on the ground.

The Eyes Have It

It might seem strange to drink up a person's tears, but certain kinds of moths have found that this is a good way to get what they need to survive. In some parts of the world, when seasons change, water and other nutrients can be hard to find.

For moths that drink tears, animals will be there year-round, with their tasty, juicy eyes just waiting for the moths to feed on them. Since this rarely hurts the other animals, maybe it's not such a bad way to live.

While most moths do not eat tears, learning about the moths that do will likely mean you look at moths in a whole new way from now on!

GLOSSARY

delicate (DEH-lih-kit) Easily broken or damaged.

fluids (FLOO-idz) Liquids.

mammals (MA-mulz) Warm-blooded animals that have backbones and hair, breathe air, and feed milk to their young.

metamorphosis (meh-tuh-MOR-fuh-sus) A complete change in form.

monsoon (mon-SOON) A strong wind from the ocean that brings a lot of rain.

mucus (MYOO-kus) A thick, slimy liquid produced by the bodies of many animals.

nutrients (NOO-tree-unts) Food that a living thing needs to live and grow.

pastures (PAS-churz) Pieces of land where animals eat plants.

protein (PROH-teen) An important element inside the cells of plants and animals.

saliva (suh-LY-vuh) The liquid in the mouth that starts to break down food and helps food slide down the throat.

savanna (suh-VA-nuh) An area of grassland with few trees or bushes.

species (SPEE-sheez) A single kind of living thing. All people are one species.

tropical (TRAH-puh-kul) Having to do with the warm parts of Earth that are near the equator.

urine (YUR-un) A liquid waste made by the body.

INDEX

A
Africa, 8–9, 14

B
butterflies, 4, 16

C
colors, 4

F
fluids, 21
foods, 5, 20

I
insects, 4

L
leaves, 5, 20

M
mammals, 6
metamorphosis, 19
mucus, 21

N
nutrients, 13, 22

P
pastures, 9
protein, 6

S
saliva, 21
scales, 4
species, 4, 8–12, 16, 19, 21

T
Thailand, 9
type(s), 5, 11, 14, 16

U
urine, 21

W
wings, 4, 18–19
wood, 5, 20

WEBSITES

Due to the changing nature of Internet links, PowerKids Press has developed an online list of websites related to the subject of this book. This site is updated regularly.Please use this link to access the list: www.powerkidslinks.com/dad/moths